2

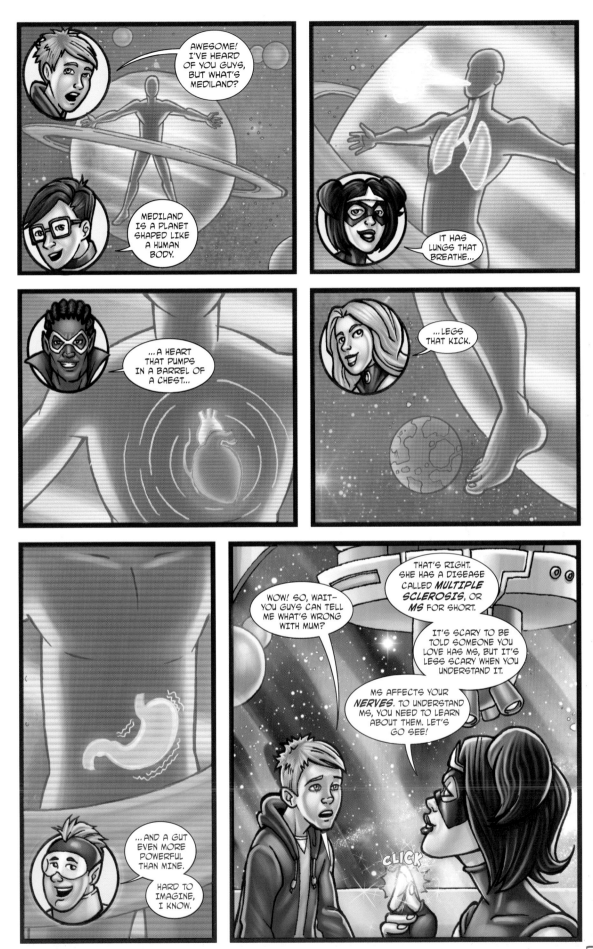

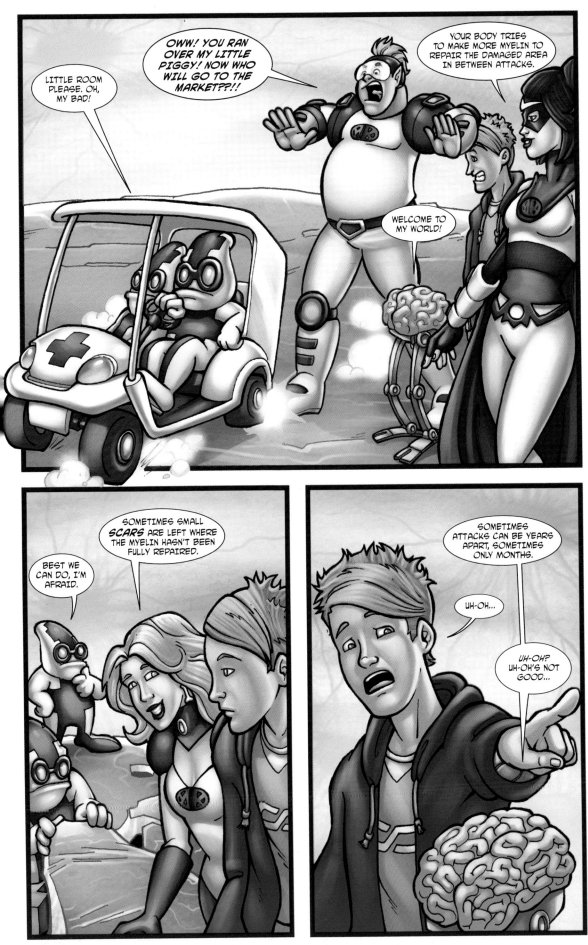

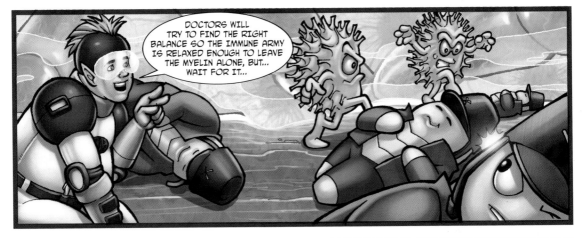

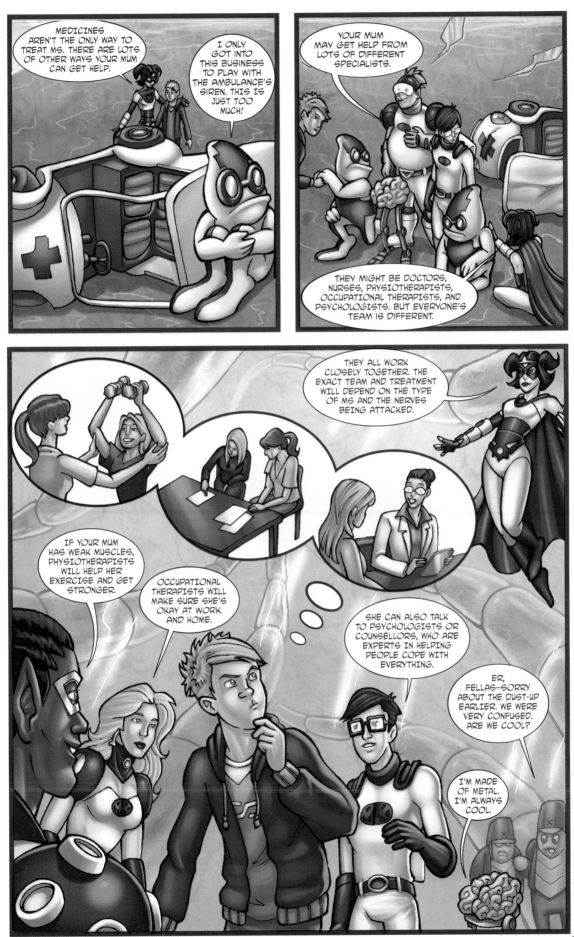

BECAUSE IT AFFECTS DIFFERENT PEOPLE IN DIFFERENT WAYS, IT CAN TAKE A WHILE FOR DOCTORS TO FIGURE OUT IT'S MS CAUSING THE SYMPTOMS.

THEY MIGHT DO AN MRI SCAN, A LUMBAR PUNCTURE TO TEST THE CEREBROSPINAL FLUID, OR AN EVOKED RESPONSE TEST TO MAKE SURE.

IN *REMITTING-RELAPSING* MS THE NERVES CAN RECOVER AND YOU FEEL BETTER AFTER AN ATTACK.

BUT IN *PROGRESSIVE* MS, THE NERVES DON'T RECOVER AND YOUR SYMPTOMS NEVER GO AWAY.

MEDICINES CAN HELP STOP ATTACKS, BUT THERE'S *NO CURE* FOR MS YET.